Contents

"The quality of a person's life
is in direct proportion to their
commitment to excellence
regardless of their chosen
field of endeavor."

-Vince Lombardi

Foreword

"Great happiness is often preceded by great dissatisfaction and great discontentment."
-Anthony Robbins

Brazilian Jiu-Jitsu is one of the most rewarding *and* challenging martial arts. There are more techniques in this art than any other martial art. And to complicate things, BJJ practitioners like to steal from other martial arts, adding even more!

This is the blessing and the curse of BJJ: you will never stop learning new techniques as the art is constantly evolving. But there is too much to choose from for the beginner!

If you try to learn everything you see- from magazines, books, videos, matches, friends, classes, and seminars, your head will spin. You will get to a position and parts of thirty different techniques will fly through your head, and you will get nothing accomplished.

There are two ways to learn anything in Jiu-Jitsu (and in life): the smart way and the hard way. Learning from someone who has already traveled the path you are on and is willing to help you is wise. Figuring it out on your own (the way I had to do it for years) is the hard way.

This book represents a smart way. If you follow the advice in this book, you will not spin your wheels nearly as much as I did.

This book was born of a lot of frustration and pain! When I first started training, no one told me "This is a beginner technique, this is intermediate, and this is advanced. You need to know this submission first, this submission second." I learned from people who studied the Gracie Basic VHS videotapes for a few months. That was tough.

Then I found more skilled practitioners who would only show parts of techniques and purposely leave out the details. After finding out they were doing that, I felt betrayed. So I started watching every video I could and going to seminars.

After a while, I had learned a lot of techniques. But I would mentally lock up while rolling- getting to a position and not do anything! My ground game was like having a house with many bricks and no cement to hold them all together. I knew a lot of techniques, but I didn't know when to use what. As an intermediate person I had forgotten more techniques than most had learned. I had no way of remembering everything I learned.

After being disorganized and frustrated for a long time, I began to organize the techniques I knew. I began to find the best ways for beginners to learn the basics. I tested many different ideas on students in classes and private lessons and saw the growth in some students explode. They were progressing more in a few months than I had in a few years!

I wished someone would have taught me in this way from the beginning. But I realized that though it was frustrating, it was in some ways a good thing as now I understand the frustration of beginning grapplers. This book is a result of that frustration- I don't want anyone to go through what I went through.

CHAPTER 1

Phases One, Two, & Three: Your Roadmap

The best way to show someone nothing is to show them everything.

The best way to learn BJJ is to break down the huge amount of techniques into small, manageable sections. If someone tells you twenty numbers, you will remember a few- usually those in the beginning and those at the end. If someone tells you a small string of numbers, like three, you will remember all three.

It has been said that the best way to teach someone nothing is to show them everything! Dividing the curriculum into three phases and subdividing the phases will help you remember the techniques you learn.

Phase One

In the beginning stage, there are four positions: the guard, mount, side mount, and back. Each position has two aspects- the defense and offense.

It is good to start with one or two moves from each position. So you can focus on learning less than sixteen moves to start. One or two attacks from the mount, and one or two defenses. And try to use these moves together in combination so they flow together. Learn one or two attacks from the guard, one or two moves from being in someone's guard, and so on.

In this phase, you will mainly focus on the closed guard.

Phase one will be completed when it starts to become second nature to do the attacks and defenses to the four basic positions (your eight to sixteen basic techniques). The goal of phase one is to bring you to a point where you can start sparring ("rolling") and not be lost as to what to do most of the time.

Rolling

When you begin live training or "rolling" you will usually be on defense most of the time. As your partners have more experience than you, you will get tapped a lot. This is natural. It doesn't mean you have no talent. It doesn't mean that you are slow. It doesn't mean that you should quit. It means you are a beginner and you are laying a necessary foundation- for your Jiu-Jitsu and your character.

The first lesson of the martial arts is humility, as humility is the necessary ingredient to learning. It is symbolized in the bow when you bring your head down and bend at your hips. If you don't cultivate humility and an eagerness to learn in the beginning, your growth will be stunted.

Many people find that the first six months or more are spent tapping. I spent over two years tapping most of the time. That was important for my game- I learned how to relax and how to see and prevent submissions.

Many people get stuck on this point. They forgot to leave their ego at the door. They focus on the frustration of losing and miss out on the lessons you can learn from every mistake you make.

There is a story about a man who wanted to become rich by finding a diamond mine. He bought a piece of property and farmed the area for years. Though he had quit his job, bought lots of equipment, and given up everything to find these diamonds, he didn't find any so he finally quit and sold the land to another person. The person who bought the land began searching, found the diamonds, and became a millionaire. The diamonds were only three feet away from where the previous owner had stopped looking!

Don't give up because you don't make anyone else tap. Winning and losing are illusions anyway. If I go and train with any of my students, they will have to tap. Does that mean that I am great? No. If I go and roll with one of the Machados, I will tap. Does that mean that I am terrible? Of course not.

The best measure of your progress is against yourself- you compare yourself today to yourself yesterday. A friend of mine once told me "All art is an argument with the past." Do not

compare yourself to others. Remember they are progressing while you are progressing.
Compare yourself to yourself.

Phase Two

At this point, you will need to add more techniques to your repertoire of techniques from the four basic positions. Phase two primarily focuses on learning the basics of the six secondary positions: quarter/turtle position, kase gatame/headlock, knee on the stomach, small package, half guard, and north south position.

As with the four primary positions, students are encouraged to learn one or two offenses and defenses from each position.

Phase two is where you begin using the open guard. There are many different open guard positions: butterfly guard, spider guard, x guard, and many others. Students are encouraged to pick one open guard and develop attacks from that position.

Learning to maintain positions is also part of phase two. How to stay in the mount when a person is trying to roll you, push your hips, or elbow escape is an example.

Another part of Phase two is defending and using strikes on the ground, if you are training Brazilian Jiu-Jitsu for self-defense.

Phase Three
At this point, attacks and defenses from the six secondary positions should be reflexive.

Depending on the school you train at, students may learn leg locks in depth, as well as more detail on all the positions. Some schools teach leg locks from the very beginning, and more traditional BJJ schools train them only at more advanced ranks.

At this stage open guards are developed much more thoroughly.

Phase One Summary
• Learn one or two attacks and one or two defenses from the mount, guard, side mount, and back.
• Drill techniques with less than 100% resistance or use 100% resistance but do not go into to full

sparring. For example, ask for 100% resistance from the mount while you try to escape. When you escape, start over or switch. Do not continue rolling.

- Focus on relaxation while doing techniques and drills.
- Learn to use basics from the closed guard.
- When you do drills, tap often and learn from your mistakes.

Phase Two Summary

- Now that you are rolling, tap often and take notes from your mistakes. Stay relaxed while you roll so you can think clearly and not burn too much energy.
- Learn basic offense and defense from the six secondary positions: quarter/turtle position, kase gatame/headlock, knee on the stomach, small package, half guard, and north south position.
- Continue to learn more from the four primary positions.
- Learn to attack in longer combinations.
- Learn how to defend your guard being passed.
- Learn how to maintain positions, shutting down escapes.
- Learn to defend and use strikes on the ground (if you are interested in self-defense).

Phase Three Summary

• Develop one or more of the open guards.
• Develop combinations in attacking the legs with ankle locks, knee bars, and toeholds.
• Find multiple set ups for basic moves. Focus on one technique for three to six months to become very proficient in it's use- like primarily going for arm bars for a few months, then chokes for a few months, then triangle, then leg attacks, then sweeps, etc.
• If you're training for self-defense, continue defending and using strikes on the ground.

"If what you are doing is not moving you towards your goals, it is moving you away from your goals."

-Brian Tracy

CHAPTER 2

The Twelve Basic Principles of Jiu-Jitsu

"Softness triumphs over hardness, feebleness over strength. What is malleable is always superior over that which is immoveable. This is the principle of controlling things by going along with them, of mastery through adaptation."

-Lao Tzu

1. Jiu-Jitsu is based on leverage.
Leverage is the ability to do a large amount of work with a small amount of energy. An example is a sweep. A person weighing 150 lbs can sweep a 250 lb person without exerting a lot of effort. Another way you could look at leverage is to see it as one person using their entire body in coordination to create a position change or a submission, as opposed to just using

just one part of your body (most commonly only using your arms.)

An example would be an armbar- the hips, arms, back, abs, and legs are all used in conjunction to put pressure on a person's elbow joint. If they don't tap, a smaller person could easily break the bigger person's arm. Jiu-Jitsu means "gentle art" because a smaller person can be effective against a larger person.

2. Good defense usually means being in a ball, offense is body straight.
When you get into a ball, it is more difficult for someone to submit you. Your chin is tight to your chest and your hands near your neck preventing a choke, your elbows are close to your body, and you have good mobility. There are also less targets for strikes as your neck, groin, stomach and face are protected.

When you are flat and someone puts their weight on you, it is often difficult to move (unless you bridge your body, like during a mount roll or "upa"). When you are doing a submission, you are putting your hips into the technique, which brings you to a position where your body is straight. This is true for the cross choke, armbar, kimura, ankle lock, guillotine, kneebar, and many others.

3. Think and act strategically.
If one game plan is not working, you need to try another plan. Otherwise you are running into a brick wall.

Let's say you are trying to choke someone from your guard. If their defense is good, start going for sweeps so you can attack from the top. If they block your sweeps, start attacking their arms.

If one thing is not working, don't force it. If you find yourself using a lot of strength, what you are doing is probably not working. The longer the match goes, the more tired you are going to get.

4. Keep your elbows close to the body while on defense, hands near your neck, and move your hips.
You can defend 90% of all submissions by doing this.

5. Be proactive- get to a better position and you will have more opportunities for submissions.

During a match one person is in control and the other is trying to catch up to the other one. The person who is in control (the one is in the better position or controlling the position) has the most opportunities for submissions. If you find yourself defending in a match, they usually are in control.

It is your job to control position so you cannot be attacked, then you can get to a better position. If you have the mount top, side top, the back, or guard, you have more submissions available to you than the other person (remember though that it is possible for the person in the inferior position to get submissions.)

This principle can be applied by the person in the inferior position. Paulo Guillobel refers to this as "the hunted becomes the hunter."

For example, your guard gets passed and you are on the side bottom. You have almost no opportunities and you are usually bearing a lot of their weight. They are attacking you with submissions and in time you will get caught.

To improve your position, you remember the basic principle of defense and get into a ball and on your side. You have proactively put yourself in a position where you cannot be submitted as easily, and in one sense you have put them on the defensive. If they do not act, you will escape. They are now playing catch up with you (you are the hunter as they have to react to what you did). Your partner finds it hard to attack and they find that they are now focused on trying to keep you in side control.

You get them back to the guard. Immediately you break their posture and begin attacking. They are now under pressure and are in danger of being submitted- you are in control.

They get their posture and break your guard. They begin to put pressure for passing. They have now taken control as you are trying to defend your guard from being passed. You can't focus on attacking, only stopping them- you are on the defensive and having to react to what they are doing. They are in control.

Jiu-Jitsu is similar to chess in many ways, but one difference is that in chess you can only make one move when it's your turn. In Jiu-Jitsu you can make as many moves as you can. In general, the more you make equals the more chances you have to improve your position or get a submission.

Jean-Jacques Machado is known to attack in machine gun fashion. He controls position so you cannot mount any kind of proactive progress. Once he gets you in a vulnerable position, he attacks until you tap.

In a well known submission grappling tournament called Abu Dabhi (ADCC), years ago there was a rule that there will be no points for the first five minutes. This was to encourage the competitors to try for submissions without worry of losing position and points. For many it had the opposite effect. They wouldn't attack until after the five minute mark.

Also, they penalized competitors for pulling people into their guard, instead of trying for a takedown. For Jean Jacques it didn't matter. He would pull them into his guard immediately and begin attacking. One year he finished all of his matches within five minutes and won the award for the most technical fighter!

6. Stay relaxed and don't burn too much energy.
Remember this is a leverage art not a strength art. The more muscle you use, the faster you burn out. You will use muscle in quick explosions, but otherwise be like water.
When you stay relaxed, you can roll for hours.

Helio Gracie had a fight with a student who was fourteen years younger, bigger and stronger than him, and they fought for almost four hours!

Besides longevity, you are more sensitive. You can feel where your partner is pushing and moving so you can respond and submit them or stop them.

In the beginning, 95% of all students are too tense and burn too much energy. A great exercise to overcome this is to set a timer and roll for twenty minutes. Agree with your partner that you are not going to stop except for submissions.

As you roll, practice deep breathing from your lower stomach (See Appendix B: Meditation Techniques.) Practice body awareness and check yourself every minute or so to see where you are holding unnecessary tension.

You can say over and over to yourself "relax, breathe." Remind yourself that if you get tapped it is good- you can learn from it. If you can't make it through twenty minutes, you are fighting too hard.

One tip I learned from David Meyer, one of Rigan Machado's black belts, is "Open hand, open mind; closed hand, closed mind."

When your hand is closed, you are generally very tense. You are straining for control and there is often fear that goes along with that.

If you open your hand, your sensitivity goes up, physical tension level goes down, and you tend to be more mentally and emotionally relaxed.

Another good way to develop relaxation as a beginner is to do what I call 30% drills. Take turns with your partner doing submissions. Do a regular roll, but you get the submission first, then your partner, then you, then your partner. You can resist your partner a little (like 30%), but you won't resist that much because it is not your turn to get the submission.

This is a great way to train your emotions and body to stay focused but relaxed when you roll. It is also a great way to train when you are injured.

7. Use your whole body when you do techniques, not just one part.
Most people usually rely on their arms for everything. Very soon your arms will get tired and you will be gasping for air.

John Machado says that American sports emphasize the upper body. Baseball, football, basketball, volleyball all mostly use the arms. In Brazil they play soccer and Capoeira- lower body activities.

From a self-defense perspective, what if a person that is much larger than you attacked you on the street? Are you going to use strength when they have much more? You have to use your brain and not just your body. Remember humans rule the world through intelligence, though humans are physically weaker than many animals on the planet.

8. To sweep someone or reverse them, you need to block out one side of their body and bring their weight forward (usually) off of their legs.
This is important to remember whenever you are trying to turn someone over. If someone is mounted on you and you want to roll them over, you must trap their hand so they don't post it out on the floor to stop the roll. You also must lift your hips as high as possible to bring their weight forward making them lighter.

This is true for most of the sweeps as well. If someone is in your guard and you want to do the scissors sweep, for example, you must grab their wrist so they don't post their hand on the floor and bring them forward so their weight is off their legs, making them lighter. If you don't, you will feel yourself using strength to bring them over, or they won't go at all.

9. Work in combination for escapes and attacks.

It is relatively easy to defend single moves. If you continue pressing with the same move that is not working, you are going to burn energy. Do not fight their strength- work around it.

If they are defending a choke, switch to an armbar, another choke, a shoulder lock, or a sweep. Attack high then low. Wherever their mind is, work around it.

10. Timing is everything.
Jiu-Jitsu literally means "gentle art." Gentle means you use your partner's energy against them. If you try to redirect their energy before they give it or after, it is too late. Then you are only using your energy.

The only way to have good timing is to make your moves reflexive. You must rep techniques and drill them enough that you do not need to think about them. That is the state called "mushin" (no mind). If you have to think, it is often too late.

11. To move someone, use as much of your body as possible against one body part of theirs.

When trying to move someone into position, don't just use your arm. Use both arms, use your arms and your legs, use your hips, use whatever you can to make yourself more powerful. You may be training with someone much bigger than you, so if you went arm vs. arm they will win, but if you use two arms and a leg vs. their arm, you will be more powerful.

I try to never use my arms to fight against someone's legs. I will use my arms, such as doing a bullfighter guard pass, but I will putting a lot of my body weight against their legs, or I will be moving my feet to change the angle. Or I will wait for them to move, and I will use that energy against them.

12. Sometimes you need to explode and fight!
Jiu-Jitsu is a technical art, but sometimes you need to commit 100% to a move- give it everything you've got.

To say that Jiu-Jitsu does not use muscle is untrue- to move any part of your body you must use strength. If you want to land any submission, you must use some explosion. If you do a move in slow motion, you will give your partner a chance to escape. If you do it quickly, you may surprise them and not give them a chance to fight the technique (but don't hurt your partner- you can explode to the first 90% of the move, but the last 10% is done slowly).

Remember not to replace the technique with strength- apply your strength through the technique.

"Flows like water, reflects like a mirror, and responds like an echo."

-The definition of Wu-Wei by Chang-Tse

CHAPTER 3

Nine Common Beginner Mistakes (Non Technical)

1. Too tense while rolling.

2. Not trusting the techniques and using brute strength- usually pushing with your arms to try to escape.

3. Waiting too long to tap.

4. Getting upset about being tapped right when it happens.

5. Getting frustrated that they are being tapped too much and they're not catching others enough.

6. When escaping, not using hips and lower body- only using your arms.

7. Not repping techniques or drilling enough- students only wanting to roll.

8. Not taking notes in class and from rolling.

9. Not reviewing basics because they always want new techniques.

"The difference between a
successful person and others
is not a lack of strength, not a
lack of knowledge, but rather
a lack of will."

-Vince Lombardi

CHAPTER 4

"Damn it!!!"

I have heard this (and worse) so many times in the dojo! Every time I hear it, I think the person yelling has missed the point. It is good to be competitive, but one of the most important things you can internalize is that **tapping is learning**. Losing is winning- as long as you learn from it.

If a beginner is winning all the time, why would they be training? They would seem to have nothing to learn. This is one of the most difficult battles you will go through. It is the battle with your ego.

Your untrained ego is your own worst enemy. You're happy when you win and frustrated when you lose. The frame of mind that will help you the most is to learn from each match.

Some people have told me "You're not going to get better unless you train with people better than you." That is false. The way you get better is to find your weak areas and improve them. It is easier when someone is better than you and tapping you, pointing out what you need to improve on, but it is possible without a better opponent.

At the end of every match you should contemplate what things you could have done better. You may have tapped your partner, but they passed your guard. You were in the mount and couldn't submit them. Or by the end of the match, you were tired.

People above your level will help you with your defense, and people below your level will help you with your offense. Those above you will be in control and are usually one step ahead of you, attacking you until you tap. You will develop your escapes to positions and submissions from their help.

Those that you are better than are trying to catch up with you during the match. They help you develop the ability to maintain a position and work in combination to get submissions.

If you feel that your offense is good and your defense needs work, let someone attack you and don't attack back. If you need to work your offense and you are not at the point where you can attack while rolling, ask someone to give you less resistance or even feed submissions to you.

School teaches us that failure is bad. You get a grade and that tells you how you did. In life, the opposite is true.

The most successful people in business, in sports, and in life are the ones with the most failures. If you define failure as a bad thing, you will not like training and you'll quit.

Thomas Edison failed over eleven thousand times before he discovered the light bulb.
Chuck Norris failed his first black belt test.
Michael Jordan didn't make the high school basketball team when he was a freshman.
Lincoln lost many, many elections before he became President.

Dan Gable, one of the greatest wrestlers (and coaches) of all time hadn't lost a single match in college. His final match was to be televised on ABC Wide World of Sports. He lost! He was very distraught. He then took that pain, disappointment, and frustration and channeled it.

He was to compete in the 1972 Olympics. The Russians were highly skilled and many expected them to take the gold. Dan Gable would wake up in the morning, feel sore from the previous days of hard work and consider taking some time off. He would then visualize the Russians training while he would be resting. Then he would train.

He won the gold at the 1972 Olympics! If he wouldn't have lost his last match in college, he may not have trained as hard. Everyone gets beat in their training, but if you let your own frustration beat you, then you have lost again!

Remember the quote "great happiness is often preceded by great dissatisfaction." Pain is often what pushes us to grow beyond our present limitations.

Another thing I would say is to balance your training. What I mean is it can be tough to tap all the time, and you know it is good for you, but it may take a little while to change your attitude about getting tapped. Roll with lower ranks to build your confidence.

You could even train with friends with little to no experience. Just make sure they know how to tap! And if they don't tap, let them go.

The Power of Persistence
Another thing to keep in mind- the single best way to get good at anything is to stick with it. The story about the tortoise and the hare is not fiction. In my first BJJ class I was the tortoise. The hares were beating me all the time. But I stuck with it, and they all quit (except one.)

Though I started slow, I really wanted to be good and I would do very well if I trained with those same people today.

Rep and Roll
An important principle of training is that you roll to find your weaknesses, then you rep techniques and drill to strengthen that area. The people that progress the fastest are those that develop this

habit. **If you learn nothing else from this book, learn this principle.**

One habit that will help tremendously is keeping a journal. Write down after a training session what you did good and what needs work.

Robert Kiyosaki, author of Rich Dad Poor Dad, says that in school if you cooperate with others on a test it is called cheating. If you do it in business and in life it is called being on the winning team. Ask your teachers and training partners for advice. Remember the squeaky wheel gets the oil!

Once you find your weaknesses, make a plan for how to improve them (see Appendix A: Goals and the Twenty Idea Method for Success.) Put the list in a place that you will see it every day. If you keep up this habit you will be shocked at how for you can progress.

Defense Comes First

A second principle of training is defense comes first. When you roll in the beginning, others will be dominating position and getting submissions.

You will probably not even have the chance to attack!

After a while, you defense will get to the point that you are seeing moves in advance and you are internalizing the principles and moves and you will start to see opportunities.

Some people get stuck at this point. They are so used to defending, when they get a chance to attack, they don't move. Your defense will develop before your offense. Accept that and do not be concerned about how often you tap.

Incremental Advances
A third principle is that of incremental advances. If you have a little niece or nephew that you only see once every year you will notice their growth. But if you see them every day, you don't see the growth.

It is the same in your advancement in grappling. You often can't see your day to day progress. If you started six months ago, think of what level you are at now. You today would beat yourself of six months ago!

Sometimes people feel like they are not progressing. But if you are training, and you are trying to improve your weak points, you are progressing.

Remember that at some point you are going to be using new techniques to your game and it will take a little time before the new techniques are as fluid as the old ones.

For example, you have a great cross choke in the guard. You decide to add a new technique to your arsenal- an armbar. You begin using it and you are not fluid with it and your timing is off. Most of the times you try it, you get your guard passed. You think "If I would just stay with the choke this wouldn't happen." But you realize that in order to grow you must take risks and step out of your comfort zone, exposing yourself to failure.

Be patient. In a few months, your arm bar is as comfortable as the choke and now you are using them together in combination, improving your offense more than double!

A good habit to develop is to tell people that tap you "thank you" and "good job." Why would you want to take someone else's accomplishment away from them? If you say "damn it," you may not learn from your mistake. If you say thanks, you are happy that your partner showed you something you can improve. They did you a favor.

In the East bamboo trees are common. The way they grow is interesting. After you plant the seed, you can give it water for the whole first year, and nothing will happen. Then the second year. Nothing. The third year it will grow one foot per day!

Your development is the same. You cannot expect immediate results. Our society encourages this mentality of immediate gratification. Train yourself to get in the habit of forgoing short term pleasure for long term success and happiness.

CHAPTER 5

"I Can't Remember All of the Techniques"

"Spectacular performances follow less spectacular preparation."

The three hardest battles to overcome in Jiu-Jitsu as a beginner are: 1) getting the right perspective on tapping, 2) learning to relax, and 3) not trying to learn too much at once.

There are thousands of techniques in Jiu-Jitsu. And there are more being created all the time. If you try to learn too much, you will not retain it. There is a rule in teaching beginners: if you want to show someone nothing, show them everything.

This is why I divided our curriculum into three phases. You will remember more if you focus on quality rather than quantity. Learn one or two moves for offense and one or two for defense from each of the four major positions and you will not get confused.

One of the most helpful things you can do as a student of Jiu-Jitsu is to write down what you know from each position. You don't need to write down everything you know, but just a few things. Write down the one or two techniques for offense and defense from the four beginning positions: mount, side mount, guard, and back. I included a basic outline for this in Appendix C (page 114).

Work these techniques until you don't have to think to do them. Once you have reached the point that they are reflexive, then add one more technique. Work this new technique into your muscle memory until it flows in combination with the other moves that you know.

Persistence and Repetition
The single most important element of success in any endeavor is persistence. You can take a non-athletic person who learns slowly and if they stay with training, in time they will be able to

defeat the large, strong, naturally gifted athlete who quit after a few months.

Training consistently at least two days per week will pay off in the long run. And take advantage of seminars- they will strengthen your game, inspire you, and deepen your commitment to Jiu-Jitsu.

Success in Jiu-Jitsu is in the details. The most important detail of your training is repetition. It is not exciting or glorious, but it is the foundation of your training.

When you first learn a technique, rep it slowly and be mindful of what you are doing. Feel the technique as you go through each step, see what you are doing, and you can say the steps out loud or mentally as you do it.

As you develop more fluency with the technique, increase the speed. The more you rep something, the less you have to think about it. If you find yourself thinking about a technique while rolling, it means you need to rep it more. When you don't need to think about the technique you can focus on the setup and timing.

Visualization / Mental Repetition

One method of repetition that is overlooked by many students is mental repetition or visualization. This includes writing notes, reading notes and books, watching videos, visualizing moves, teaching, and watching matches. Visualization can be as effective as physical repetition, if you apply good concentration.

When I studied Capoeira (a Brazilian acrobatic dance martial art) I had a hard time learning the gymnastic parts. Because I had bad knees, I couldn't do many repetitions like I could do with other martial arts techniques.

There was one move in particular that was very difficult, called *au bachiva*. You stand on one arm as one leg does a downward delivered roundhouse kick. I tried this move many times and the impact of landing back on one leg was bothering my knee. So I spent one week visualizing myself doing the technique whenever I had a chance.

The next week I tried the move and got it the first time!

There was an American P.O.W. in Vietnam for several years. He was locked in a tiger cage and spent his days mentally playing golf. He even visualized tying his shoes. When he returned to the states, his golf score had improved though he hadn't touched a club in years!

Concentration

Some people do not focus their minds deeply while doing repetition. If you concentrate deeply on the technique during repetition, your learning curve will shorten dramatically.

Bruce Lee said the best preparation for an event is the event itself. If you are interested in improving your concentration, the best way is to concentrate! This is one reason why martial artists meditate- when you meditate you are practicing concentration. See Appendix B for a list of meditation techniques.

Our culture does not encourage the development of concentration. This is one of the many subjects that should be taught in school as it is a necessary element of learning anything.

Our world is designed around convenience and speed. When television became popular in the 1950s, the scene on the screen changed every ten to fifteen seconds. Now it changes every two to three seconds!

Learning anything of value is neither fast nor convenient. It requires patience, bearing occasional frustration, boredom, mental overload, and riding out plateaus in your development (feeling like you aren't moving forward even though you are working hard).

Success in grappling comes with a price. If you are willing to pay it, you will reap the rewards.

The Three Styles of Learning
Some learn Jiu-Jitsu fast and others slow. One reason for this is some have found a method of how to learn things. Most people are not even conscious that they have a learning style, but everyone has one of three styles: auditory, visual, or kinesthetic. Most people usually have

one dominant style, but some use a combination of styles.

Auditory learners hear directions and repeat the steps out loud or mentally as they do the technique.

Visual learners have a picture of the technique in their mind that they try to recreate.

Kinesthetic learners like to feel the technique being done to them and then feel the technique as they do it to their partner.

Everyone has a dominant learning style but it is possible to combine all three methods to learn a technique.

For example, you have just been shown the cross choke from the guard. You remember the steps: cross grab the collar with your right hand, reach your left hand in deep so it nearly touches your other hand, pull their head to your chest, and bend your wrists into their neck. You repeat these steps aloud as you practice with your partner. You visualize what the technique looks like and try to match what you are doing with how the instructor demonstrated it. You feel your first hand reaching in deep, then you feel your second hand in deep, and you feel their head touching your chest as your elbows touch your ribs.

The fastest way to learn techniques is visually. Repeating steps to yourself takes a little time but seeing a picture is immediate. If you would like to develop a visual memory, begin visualizing techniques.

I used to be an auditory learner (though I didn't know it) and I struggled every time I was taught a new technique. I didn't have a method of learning.

Over time, after much frustration, I began to visualize techniques and began learning much quicker. Eventually I was able to see a technique once or twice and store it in memory without repetition! This is really useful in grappling as there are so many techniques to learn.

"Nothing great was ever
achieved without
enthusiasm."

-Ralph Waldo Emerson

CHAPTER 6

One Secret That Will Increase Your Defense By 100%

The secret of success in any endeavor is persistence.

John Machado told me to not be a master of kamikaze escapes. Don't let your arm get caught and accomplish a daring escape.

Remember that BJJ is not a sport- it is a form of self-defense. A joint lock on the street would not be done slow with control as the joint reached it's limit. It would be done quickly, like a punch. There would be not time to do a fancy escape.

It takes a long time to learn several escapes for all of the different submissions. There are new submissions created every day from all over the world! To learn the escapes from every one would take a long time. I have something that is much simpler.

In health, prevention is better than the cure. It takes planning and discipline, but it is easier to prevent most diseases than cure them. And if someone has a disease, it is generally easier to cure the earlier you catch it.

The secret of defending submissions is simple. In order for someone to choke you, they have to have a hand near your neck. In order for someone to attack your elbow or shoulder, they have to touch your arm.

The secret of preventing submissions is awareness. If you touch my neck, I am going to defend my neck: bringing my hand to my face or securing your arm that is on my neck. If you touch my arm, I am going to bring it close to my body and bring that side of my body to the floor.

If you just keep your arms in and your neck protected, you are still in danger. So while you are protecting yourself, you need to move your hips. That means bumping, shrimping, reverse shrimping, and/or going belly down. You need to change position so you are no longer in a position where they can attack you.

The next time you roll with someone better than you, keep your hands near your neck, your elbows close to your body, move your hips, and see how much longer it takes for them to tap you. You do not need to know thirty or forty escapes to submissions. You know one principle that will take you much, much further.

There was a farmer walking in the village marketplace. He accidentally knocked over the dinner plate of a Samurai onto the floor. The Samurai became enraged and challenged the farmer. The farmer offered to pay for the meal and apologized profusely, but the Samurai said they must duel, saying that if he tried to hide he would find him. He said the duel would occur in one week.

The farmer sought out the local sword master. The sword master said, "You have to get used to the fact that you are going to die. I will show you one stance, one cut, and at least you will kill him when he strikes you."

The farmer thought and practiced all week. He mentally prepared for his own death. He met the Samurai and got into his stance. He stared with great focus at the Samurai. The Samurai moved forward, trying to get him to react. The farmer stood motionless. The Samurai circled left, circled left. After one hour the Samurai stepped back and said "There is no opening for me to attack without getting struck myself. You show absolute concentration and no fear. You have the spirit of the Samurai. For me, our problem is over."

The farmer's friends came over to him to congratulate him. The farmer remained in his stance as he was still so focused, without anything clouding his mind.

CHAPTER 7

Focus

In my own training I have found that when I have specific things I am trying to achieve, I progress much faster.

Remember that the point of repping techniques is to be able to do them without thinking, so you can do them in live rolling. If you rep something and never try to do it in rolling, you are just doing the same techniques that you always have been doing. In that way your Jiu-Jitsu won't growing.

Have you heard how many people in personal development define insanity? It's doing the same thing over and over, and expecting different results.

So how do you take something that you have been repping and make it part of your "working vocabulary?'

One of the best ways is to start matches from the position that you are trying to work from. As a beginner, you are mainly doing to be working defense. At some point, you are going to want to focus on your side control escapes. For a few weeks or more, start all of your matches from the side bottom (a lot of people won't mind starting in a superior position!)

Another option is to remind yourself before every match what you want to achieve. This does not work as well, because it is very easy to get distracted and lose your focus.

I had a student years ago that wanted to improve his mount escapes. He asked me questions about how to escape, he repped the escapes in combination a lot, and then he started every match in mount bottom for a few months.

After a while, no one could stay mounted on him! He took his weakest area and made it his strongest with only a few months of focused training.

CHAPTER 8

Injuries

Injuries happen in training, but they can be minimized. Most people get injured because of three reasons:

1. They waited too long to tap. They didn't want to accept that they made a mistake and they won't take responsibility for it. This is completely unnecessary and may cost you weeks or months of training.

2. They are too tense. If someone gets you in an armbar and you defend by tensing your arm as tight as you can, your partner will put a lot of pressure on your arm. If you decide to let go or your muscles give up, your partner is still applying a lot of pressure and you may get injured.

The proper way to defend a lock is with proper technique, using as much of your body as possible, not just the muscles of your arm.

3. They get hurt by a beginner- beginners often get overexcited and have poor control. When you work with a beginner, it is good not to do 100% live sparring. They will sometimes get overexcited or scared and fly into submissions very fast.

It is better to do drills with beginners. You have to be very watchful of beginners as they don't mean to hurt you, they just don't know what they are doing.

If you are a beginner and you are not sure about your control, remember one rule. You can go into the first part of a submission fast, but the last 25% should be done slow. If you do an armbar, do not bring their arm immediately to one hundred and eighty degrees. Get their arm a bit past a right angle and apply your hips and back slowly to bring their arm to one hundred and eighty degrees.

You are giving them more of a chance to escape, but you are learning to control the technique and you are showing regard for your partner that will be reflected back to you when you are having the technique done to you.

How to Relax When Rolling
The chance of injury is higher when you are nervous. And when you are in such close contact with someone, other people will feel your tension and may become more nervous themselves. It is important that you breathe deeply with your lower stomach to relax.

Appendix B has breathing and meditation techniques for you to practice. Besides learning how to relax at will, they will also help you develop body awareness. As you roll, you will start seeing where you are holding tension.

The best thing you can do to help another person calm down and calm yourself down, especially if you are rolling with someone you have never trained with before, is to complement them during the roll. "Good try," "Nice sweep," "That was close," are things you can say to let your partner know that you are not in adrenal stress mode, or some crazy person, and they don't need to fear you!

Other Ways to Prevent Injuries

The first is warming up and light stretching. A good way to warm up is to spend a few minutes shrimping, or doing anything that gets your heart rate up. This is one of the reasons that many academies spend the first half hour doing jogging and other calisthenics.

Lifting weights can be helpful in preventing injuries. It isn't necessary to lift huge amounts of weight, but strengthening the muscles will help protect your joints. In my experience, people who lift heavy weights for many years tend to have many joint problems, so be smart about lifting weights.

Some people find Yoga helpful as it will stretch and strengthen the entire body, as well as helps you develop body and mental/emotional awareness. For more than 5 years I had a lot of problems with my lower back, and doing Yoga was the only thing that helped me.

Now, in order to keep my spine in alignment and my back strong, I do a series of postures very similar to Yoga that are part of the Foundation Program (search *Foundation* on Amazon.com by Eric Goodman and Peter Park.)

Swimming also is a great exercise. You will stretch and strengthen many areas of your body as long as you are doing different swimming strokes. Swimming will also improve your cardiovascular endurance as there is pressure on your lungs, plus when you go completely under water and you have to hold your breath.

Some people have found going to a good chiropractor is helpful. Roger Machado told me something that his Yoga instructor told him: "You are as young as your back is strong and healthy." Most people have bad posture- while walking, standing, driving, sitting at a desk, and watching television.

And one of the most important things you can do is to listen to your body. On the days that you feel very tight or weak in a certain area- do not do any live rolling or sparring. Do drills and rep techniques.

Training hard every time you come to class is not good. It doesn't mean you aren't a tough guy if you don't roll. I have seen many tough guys trying to impress other people to maintain their reputation and overdo training. They eventually have to take time off and sometimes quit. Don't be another tough guy sitting on the bench. Be honest with yourself and be balanced.

A final note on injuries: they can teach you balance. I have seen many students realize that they are too tense when rolling from being injured.

What happens right after the injury is that they have to take time off. When they do come back to training, they can't go 100%. They roll with a different mindset and often have tell me that they could see so much more of what was going on. They realize that fear causes them to have a lot of tension in their body, which burns more energy and ends up making them tired. And that extra tension kills their sensitivity.

What I find interesting is that students who find they have this tendency on the mat have the same tendency in life. Fear stands for **F**alse **E**xpectations **A**ppearing **R**eal.

Many years ago I heard a monk say that all of our motivations boil down to one of two things: love, or fear. That blew my mind as I started to realize how many things I did out of fear!

Many people don't realize that it is fear that prevents them from enjoying relationships, taking chances, and getting the most out of life! This is one way that training will change you from the inside out.

The word *dojo* means "Place where the ego undergoes transformation." When you begin to battle fear in your life and destroy your own worst enemy, it is like taking off a winter coat that you are wearing on a hot summer day.

You feel free and relaxed and you wonder why you had that draped over you. It was not necessary. It was only your perception that something would hurt you. We are often so afraid to be exposed and be honest with ourselves, but that is the only way we experience mental, emotional, and spiritual freedom.

CHAPTER 9

Strategies for Growth in Brazilian Jiu-Jitsu

"Jiu-Jitsu is a game of chess."

1. **Cycle repetition with rolling**. One purpose of rolling is to find out where you are weak so you can strengthen that area. Once you find an area, learn the techniques and strategies to strengthen your game.

Once you have repped the techniques that will make your weak area stronger, then go back to rolling and see if you have improved that area. If you have, search out the next area.

People that roll too much and don't work technique get sloppy and do not develop technical Jiu-Jitsu.

People that do not roll or "go live" don't know where their weak areas are and often have poor timing and are weak with combinations.

2. **When learning new techniques, start with 0% resistance and work your way up**. When you are first learning, go slow and do the technique step by step. After you can do the steps smoothly, drill the technique with speed many times. After that, you can start asking your partner for light resistance so you start developing the sensitivity and timing to make the technique work.

If possible, find another technique that works in combination with the one you have worked and have your partner resist a little.

After you have gone through this process, try it in rolling. You can start with someone who is below your level. Then try it against people who are at your level. Sometimes students drill a technique and start trying it out on higher ranks. After it fails several times, they stop trying to use it.

If you are developing proficiency with the technique on people below or at your level, try it on those above you.

Remember that when you roll with someone who is better than you, you are usually on defense most of the time, so you may find that if you are trying an offensive technique, you may not be able to even get into the position to try the technique you are working on.

If you stay with a technique or combination, you can become very proficient. Just because you are not a black belt does not mean you cannot be a black belt in a technique.

Roger Machado had a white belt student who was black belt level in the triangle. He would go to a tournament and win five out of seven matches with this technique. In the dojo, he would catch many high ranks.

3. **Share what you are learning with others**. This is the principle of good selfishness or the selfish/unselfish principle: the person you are helping will be happy that you are sharing, but you may get more out of it. You may remember

10% of what you hear, but you will remember 90% of what you teach!

4. Take notes in class and from rolling. One of Bruce Lee's students, Sifu Richard Bustillo often tells his classes "Those who don't take notes work for those who do!" Note takers get much more out of a class and rolling than those who don't.

5. Visualize techniques while not in the dojo. Write notes from class and on your rolling, watch videos, watch people roll, visualize techniques, and teach others. If you do this enough you will develop a visual memory and you will not require as much repetition of techniques.

This is what happened to me- I used to rep techniques endlessly and still struggled. I began visualizing and being more mentally engaged while repping techniques, and my Jiu-Jitsu improved immensely!

6. Find the moves you are good at and work them in combinations with other moves, with

different setups and work the timing. In the highest levels of any art form, athletes are usually unstoppable with one move. In wrestling, you see some that have an amazing double leg. In Jiu-Jitsu it is important to find a few things you are good at and keep them as a core of your game. Setups, timing, and combinations are what make you good at a technique, which is a lot more than just knowing the technique.

7. **Train consistently**. You will get out of training what you put into it. Write down your goals for training and review them daily. Train at home when you don't have time to make it to the dojo (this includes mental repetition and visualization).

Get to know others at the school so you feel more comfortable and you will miss training more if you miss practice.

One thing that our culture does not encourage is sacrifice. Sacrifice is necessary to attain excellence in and endeavor. You cannot live a life that is normal and achieve more than what others achieve.

Keith Hafner, a successful martial arts school owner who at one time had more than eight hundred students, used to only have one hundred students and struggled. When he decided he was going to take his life and income to the next level, he had to sacrifice three things he really enjoyed: politics, sports, and chess.

You only have so many waking hours in a day- every minute you spend mindlessly watching t.v. or involved in other time wasting activity is time that you are not investing in yourself. I am not saying it is wrong to watch t.v.- it is good to have diversions, but many people spend more than an hour per day- that will not lead to victories on the mat or in life.

Those who have attained the most success have had the most failures.

CHAPTER 10

Basics

Repetition is the mother of all skills.

The most common thing you will hear martial arts instructors telling students is "Work the basics. The basics are the most important." What are the basics in Brazilian Jiu-Jitsu?

I do feel that there are techniques that every student should know very well. But rather than giving you a list of moves, I will share a concept.

A basic move is a move that you use the most often.

The most important basic technique is the hip escape. This body movement is an important part of many, many, many Jiu-Jitsu techniques. If you practice this move often, you will strengthen your foundation.

The second most important move is the hip bump or bridging (called "upa" in Brazil, this is where you are lying flat on your back and you bring your feet in close to your body and lift your hips up from the floor). This is also found in many techniques.

Notice that both of these basic movements involve the hips? It is common to hear in Jiu-Jitsu "move your hips" and "use your hips." The hips are the center of the body. Connected to your quadriceps, the strongest muscles in the body, they are the most important area to learn to move.

As far as techniques, the basics are going to be slightly different for everybody. For example, a larger person might find that moves that work better for them are moves that you can use your body weight and not have to move very much. From the side mount top they may like the americana and kimura.

A smaller person may not have as much success with these moves. They may prefer an armbar and chokes. You have to find techniques that work for your body type.

I'm not saying that a big guy can't or shouldn't do armbars or a smaller guy can't or shouldn't do kimuras, I am saying that it is helpful to recognize what techniques will fit your game. All beginners should learn all of the basic submissions, no matter what their size and weight is.

Another example of everyone's basics being different is side mount escapes. Different instructors will have different methods for escaping the side mount. One will tell you that you need to put your far arm under their far armpit. Another will say you need to put that same hand on the near side of their neck.

Another will tell you to put it on their front arm. All methods are correct, and none are perfect. But what is for sure is escaping from the side mount is something that you must know how to do. It happens often and is therefore a basic.

One of the most important basic skills you must have is using the guard and passing the guard. The guard is the most important position in Brazilian Jiu-Jitsu and most matches hinge on the guard. If you can pass the guard, you will be able to attack. If you can't, there will be a lot of pressure on you and you may get swept or tap.

There are a lot of different basics you can use to attack from and pass the guard, but you must be fluent in your use of a few.

When a teacher says "learn the basics" there is more to a basic than the technique itself. They are telling you to learn the technique so it is ingrained in your muscle memory and you do not have to think about it when you are rolling. That frees you up to focus on two things: the set up, and the timing.

Beginners find quickly that just knowing a technique is not enough. You may be able to execute a technique without resistance and not even come close when you get resistance. That is because you are missing the set up and you don't have a sense for the timing.

A set up is where a move starts from, the launching pad. An example is an armbar from the guard. If you do not get someone slightly bent forward and their elbow on or above your upper stomach, you can't get an armbar. This is called breaking their posture, another important basic drill.

To learn how to get someone into position is as important as the technique itself. If you don't do it, the armbar will not happen.

A common way to set up a technique is with another technique. An example is setting up an armbar from the guard with a cross choke. When you put one hand in their collar, the person you are attacking will often defend the choke with their hand. When they do that, they often bend forward slightly and leave their elbow away from their body- exactly what you need to get the armbar.

If you get the arm to your upper stomach and you take too long to execute, you may miss it. If you move before their arm gets into position, you will miss it. This is one of the basic principles of Jiu-Jitsu: timing. The right move executed at the wrong time will not work.

And often one of the key components of timing is sensitivity. If you are relaxed enough to feel what your partner is doing, you can feel when their weight starts to shift so you can land the sweep you are setting up.

If you are not connected to your partner, and aren't paying attention to their movement, you may just try your sweep when they are not off balance, and it doesn't work.

There are two laws of success:

1) You must pay full price.

2) You must pay in advance. A farmer never goes to his field and says "Give me wheat and I will sow seeds!" You cannot expect success without putting the necessary time in. And the only way to develop patience is to practice it!

CHAPTER 11

Rank Advancement

I have seen adult students turn into children when they don't get the belt that they think they deserve. They will switch to a new school, quit completely, or whine and complain.

When I went from blue to black belt under Rigan Machado, I did not have a curriculum to follow. Sometimes he would give me advice about what I needed to do next, and sometimes he wouldn't. When I look back at it, I could say that I wished things were more organized, but Rigan's often baffling methods of doing things helped me practice patience, trust, nonattachment to rank, and maturity.

As a blue belt I was regularly flying from Michigan to California to train for a week to three weeks at a time. At that time, there were only handful of blue belts and purple belts in the entire state of Michigan. As a business owner and practitioner, getting my purple belt was a big deal.

I rolled with one of Rigan's tough purple belts, Ryan Gregg. He told me that I should definitely get my purple. He said that he would talk to Rigan about it and let me know.

I was anxious to hear what Rigan had to say, and I had to wait a few days to get my response.

"No" Ryan Gregg said.

"Did he say anything else, like why, or what I need to do?" I asked.

"Nope."

I could have went through a downward spiral of feeling angry at Rigan, sorry for myself, and other negative thoughts and emotions. But I had a conversation with myself:

"Rigan is your teacher, do you trust him? He is the high level practitioner, and you are a blue belt. Do you really think you know better than he does?"

I decided to trust my teacher, be patient, keep working hard, and not focus on the belt.

I thought about it and knew that Rigan has a lot going on. My purple belt is way more important to me than to him, and I know that squeaky wheels get oiled, so I decided to have a conversation with him.

I believe that most relationships have problems because of lack of constructive communication. I told Rigan, "I would like to get my purple belt sometime, but I only want it if I deserve it. Whether I get it now or later, I ultimately just want to get better. Sometime before I go back to Michigan, could you let me know what I need to do to get better?"

"Ok my friend," he said smilingly.

Before I flew back, he asked me to roll with one of his top purple belts. My anxiety went up as I knew this purple belt was a monster.

Soon after we started rolling, the purple belt started to sweep me and I immediately dropped into a kneebar and the monster tapped.

After we were done, Rigan told the class, "Everyone against the wall." That meant he was about to award me my purple belt.

At that time, getting my purple belt was a really big deal. I actually had balloons and streamers hanging in the dojo when I got back!

Earning my purple belt from him was a big accomplishment for me, but I am more proud that my traditional martial arts training from Kung Fu kept me centered and I kept the right attitude.

CHAPTER 12

Getting Your Blue Belt

In general, if you are wondering where you are at in terms of rank, you can generally measure your rolling. If you are a white belt, see how you do with other blue belts.

Take into consideration age, weight, and strength. If you are a 23 year old, 220 lb ex collegiate wrestler, and you regularly beat a 150 lb, 40 year old blue belt, you do not necessarily need to start a campaign for getting your blue belt.

If a Brazilian Jiu-Jitsu black belt beats a Sambo black belt, it doesn't mean that they should be a Sambo black belt as well. To earn a rank in any martial art, you should know the curriculum for that rank, and be using those basics in live training.

Here is a checklist to give you a general idea of where you are at:

1. You need to know the basic techniques, and be using them fluently. You should be starting to use the basics in combination.

2. You should not be making basic mistakes, like extending your arms and pushing people off of the mount, giving up your back, etc…

3. You should be able to do 4 or 5 rounds, for five minutes each, without getting too tired. If you are using too much strength, and/or staying too tense, you won't last.

4. You should be training at least 2 days per week.

5. You should be able to hold your own with many blue belts, and should be able to submit most of the white belts that you train with.

Every school has slightly different requirements, but if you feel that you are ready, you may want to have a conversation with your instructor. Be respectful, listen as least as much as you talk, and be humble.

If you do not get promoted as fast as you want, enjoy being a tough white belt!

If you feel you deserve your blue belt therefore have an issue with your instructor, do not talk to lots of other students about it. And do not go online and complain. That is cowardly!

An adult has adult conversations with other adults. A coward tells everyone else but the person they are having a problem with how they really feel.

Most of the time that a student feels they deserve a rank, the student is wrong. Remember that part of training is learning patience and humility.

Remember that everyone's journey is different. Some people spend a long time at white belt, and less at blue. I spent two and a half years at white, five years at blue, around two at purple, and around one and a half at brown. In the end, it will all balance out.

CHAPTER 13

Garbage In, Garbage Out; Good In, Good Out (GIGO)

"I've never known a man worth his salt who, in the long run, deep down in his heart, didn't appreciate the grind, the discipline. There is something really good in men who yearn for discipline."

-*Vince Lombardi*

There is a rule in physical health: what you put into your body is what you get out. If you eat a lot of processed foods, drink alcohol, caffeine, smoke, avoid fruits and fresh vegetables, etc… you will have low levels of energy and health. You will be nervous, often sick, overweight, and often depressed.

When you put good food and live a healthy lifestyle, the benefits far outweigh the cost.

There is a concept in personal development: everything is equally hard. Working out takes discipline and can be hard, but being overweight is hard.

Quitting smoking is hard, but suffering from all of the harmful effects of smoking is hard.

Eating healthy can be hard, but so is eating unhealthy and feeling low levels of energy and guilt for not caring for yourself.

Bad habits are easy to develop and hard to live with. Good habits are hard to develop and easy to live with.

The same applies to your mental and emotional health. If you regularly consume a toxic diet of worry, fear, anger, lack of mental discipline and focus, lack of commitment, you will reap the fruits of no control over you mind or emotions.

Your spirit will be agitated and you experience little peace.

What you do outside the dojo affects your performance in the dojo, as your life in the dojo affects your life outside. If you are practicing discipline of your body, mind, and emotions outside of the dojo, you will find disciplining yourself inside the dojo easier. When you practice discipline inside the dojo, discipline in your daily life outside the dojo is easier. Your "discipline muscles" are stronger.

A student that finds many difficulties in training is often making their first efforts in a long time to control themselves. Controlling your mind is like training a child to behave. If you haven't trained them in their first fifteen years of life and you decide one day to discipline them, you are going to have a fight on your hands. If you do not regularly discipline yourself, whenever you need to do it, it will be difficult.

Training martial arts is preparing for war. I don't mean physical war, but within yourself.

In Islam there is a term, "Jihad." It means holy war. To zealots it means kill somebody. To those with wisdom it means waging war on your bad qualities to allow your potential to be expressed.

When you begin the battle with your mind, you may find tremendous resistance. Years of habit may not be in your favor. You may find strong tendencies to make excuses, blame others, give in to frustration, get distracted, lack of commitment, etc. The good news is that the more you try to discipline yourself, the easier it gets.

If you never lifted weights and one day walk into a gym and try to bench press your body weight, you may find yourself trapped under the bar! If you start with a small weight and consistently increase it as your strength increases, after a while you will lift double your body weight.

The mind is more powerful than the body. As you practice discipline in your daily life, your mental muscles will strengthen. You will gain greater control over yourself. You will find it easy and exciting to set and achieve goals.

As you build your confidence, you will find yourself having the expectation that you will achieve your goal. This is one of the ways that martial arts develops confidence- when you achieve a reasonable level of proficiency, you prove to yourself that you are capable of achieving something difficult, and more likely to achieve other goals in the future.

Modern American life does not encourage discipline. It encourages convenience, comfort of the body, and everything fast.

We are overloaded on the sensory level and in material comforts. I am not against these things, but when it gets out of balance, you suffer.

One hundred years ago people may have suffered from hunger, now people overeat. People may have worked very hard physically then, now they don't get enough exercise.

Modern life can easily weaken the spirit. You may be wondering "How do I practice discipline in my daily life?"

In the East there are many ancient traditions that develop control of the mind. I have included a list of a few tools and a short description of each activity:

Affirmations: repeating a phrase over and over until your subconscious believes it. For a salesman that fears rejection, he may repeat "I am the best" for twenty minutes every day on his way to work.

By the time he gets to work he feels energetic and excited because his mind is beginning to believe that he is the best at what he does.

He now smiles more, is more relaxed, is more confident, and builds repoire with prospective clients much more easily. A grappler that suffers from low confidence can repeat "I am in control" to themselves before or during a match. Or someone that is too tense whole rolling repeats "I am calm, relax."

Camping, canoeing, and getting out into nature: it is amazing how free you feel without phones ringing, appointments, having to be somewhere at all times, no t.v., cars, alarm clocks, etc. Modern life can fray your nerves and getting away from technology and the modern schedule is a great way to revitalize your nervous system.

Controlling the senses: This means to not give in to the incessant demands for comfort of the body. This will develop mental toughness.

You may take a shower that isn't hot, walk outside without enough clothes to remain warm, give up sweets for a period of time, etc.

Fasting: abstaining from food and only drinking water or juice for a day or more. Native Americans would often do this before war to help clear the mind and prepare for their battle.

Meditation: the art of stilling the body and focusing the mind on a single point.

Mental and emotional fasts: spend periods of time that you will not allow yourself to indulge in worry, fear, anger, or any negative emotion that you habitually fall into.

Practicing silence: this may seem like a strange thing to do, but it is extremely powerful. You don't realize how much or energy is going outward to the world and not into our selves.

Take a half or a full day and don't say anything to anyone! It is amazing the level of mental stillness you can create.

Gandhi used to take every Monday as a day for silence. He was the leader of India and he had tremendous demands on himself. But he felt that if he didn't take care of himself, he would have nothing to give his country.

Stephen Covey says "Do not kill the goose that lays the golden egg." You are the goose! You must take care of yourself- for the sake of yourself and others.

A really powerful habit is to feed your mind continuously with positive information. Listening to personal development information, reading non-fiction books, learn about the lives of successful people, surround yourself with positive minded and successful people, constantly set and review goals, and avoid negative people and energy drainers.

Develop the habit of constantly improving yourself in different areas. Live outside of your comfort zone. Strengthen your learning muscles. Learn a different language, how to cook a certain type of food, learn to play an instrument, study history, learn a new physical skill like rock climbing- anything that interests you and will challenge you.

The term in Japanese is "kohai," which means eager student. It you apply this attitude in martial arts and in life, you will be on fire for life. You will wake up excited for all the things you are excited about, as opposed to waking up and feeling the burden of the life you have created.

Remember if you don't like your life, you made it this way. Whether it was a lack of planning, laziness, wanting attention or martyr complex, you created it.

One of the most beautiful things about living in America is you are surrounded with opportunities. You cannot be stopped if you want to change your life. You have to make the decision then begin paying the price of success. The same way you achieve success in martial arts is the same way you achieve it in life: set a goal, be persistent, and be patient.

There was a carpenter who was planning on retiring. He stopped taking pride in his work. He found himself using shoddy materials, not being thorough, and frequently looking at his watch.

He told his boss he was going to leave, and his boss asked him to build one more house.

The carpenter reluctantly agreed. He made the house without pride and effort. When he finished, he told his boss he was done. The boss said "I have a surprise for you" and handed him the key to the house that he just built.

Every day we are building the house that is our life. We can just pass the time, or we can take pride and live with passion.

CHAPTER 14

The Path of the Warrior

"If the mind is as clear as a mirror, there is no need of a sword."

-Miyamoto Musashi

To call Jiu-Jitsu a sport is to not see the big picture. A sport is for points, trophies, public acclaim (ego), or money.

An art is much greater. It is about your own personal development and happiness. It is about expressing your potential.

Trophies and outer rewards measure your performance in relation to others. Art is comparing yourself today to yourself last month and demanding progress.

One of the greatest benefits of training Jiu-Jitsu is confidence. As you develop confidence, you dissipate inner fears and find yourself not threatened by others. As you are not threatened by others, you don't feel the need to put up barriers around yourself to protect yourself. You can be open with others because you see they can't hurt you.

At the highest level, you develop a desire to serve others with your strength. Training often begins as a need for self-defense and transforms into a much more noble and beautiful experience. You start with a desire to protect yourself, and you can evolve into a desire to develop yourself and others.

The greatest battles are not on the mat. They exist in your own consciousness- the fight between fear and peace, anger and forgiveness, jealousy and honesty, moodiness and discipline, egotism and humility. Some of the world's greatest warriors never threw a punch or swung a sword.

Gandhi is a great example. He refused to use violence in his fight for the independence of India from the British. He believed that the only way to achieve true freedom was in developing mental and emotional maturity. He believed that controlling one's self was a far greater tool than controlling another person.

He said that the British would leave India as friends and not beaten down enemies, and that came true.

He was assigned bodyguards to watch his every move as the British suspected him of being a criminal. Before long the bodyguards were sending Gandhi Christmas cards as they saw his nature. He led millions of people to stand up for what they believed in and willing to sacrifice even their bodies for truth.

Mother Theresa personally lifted over forty two thousand people off the streets of Calcutta. She influenced her Sisters in the Missions of Charity to do the same. Her inner and outer struggles were immense, yet she persevered and was absolutely passionate about her work, and changed the lives of millions.

If you continue training until the end of your life, and at the end of your life you look back and say "I never used what I learned in a real situation- I never choked or hit anybody to defend myself," that would be sad. Your greatest victories are on the battlefield of your consciousness. Apply the spirit of fearlessness, commitment, humility, patience, timing, strategic thinking, and intuition to your daily life. And use it serve others.

THE TWO WOLVES : A CHEROKEE STORY

A young boy came to his Grandfather, filled with anger at another boy who had done him an injustice.

The old Grandfather said to his grandson, "Let me tell you a story. I too, at times, have felt a great hate for those that have taken so much, with no sorrow for what they do. But hate wears you down, and hate does not hurt your enemy. Hate is like taking poison and wishing your enemy would die. I have struggled with these feelings many times."

"It is as if there are two wolves inside me; one wolf is good and does no harm. He lives in harmony with all around him and does not take offence when no offence was intended. He will only fight when it is right to do so, and in the right way. But the other wolf, is full of anger. The littlest thing will set him into a fit of temper."

"He fights everyone, all the time, for no reason. He cannot think because his anger and hate are so great. It is helpless anger, because his anger will change nothing. Sometimes it is hard to live with these two wolves inside me, because both of the wolves try to dominate my spirit."

The boy looked intently into his Grandfather's eyes and asked,

"Which wolf will win, Grandfather?"

The Grandfather smiled and said, "The one I feed."

APPENDIX A

Goals and the Twenty Idea Method for Success

"If what you are doing is not moving you toward your goals, it is moving you away from your goals."

-Brian Tracy

I learned the twenty idea method from Brian Tracy, the well known personal development author and speaker.

Do not discard this idea because it is simple. The best things in life are often overlooked because they are simple.

Remember success is in the details. Everyone wants glory but few are willing to put in the daily work to be great.

I have heard that when all the Gracies lived in Brazil they used to train five hours per day. Rickson Gracie, the undisputed champion of the family (after Rolls had died), used to train eight hours per day!

Larry Bird was hired to do a commercial for a soft drink company. He was supposed to miss a shot and say a certain line. It took him nine times to miss the shot! He had trained so much to make it that it took a real effort for him to miss.

20 Idea Method

Write down twenty ideas to improve your Jiu-Jitsu. Don't edit the ideas. You may come up with ten good ideas. This will help focus the power of your conscious and subconscious mind. Post this list where you can see it and look at it every day.

Written Goals

There was a study done of a graduating class at Harvard University in the 1950's. Researchers tracked the income levels of that class over a twenty year period, and they found something very interesting. The 3% who had written their goals down for their career and income level made more than the other 97% of the class *combined.*

The path to success in anything is not always exciting. The core of success is repetition, review, and analyzing rolling. Writing your goals down and reviewing them often is not exciting, but it will focus your subconscious and conscious mind.

Anything worth having is worth working for. And the greater the thing is that you want, the more that it will take to achieve it. Few people are willing to put in the work to achieve what they want. They live in the world of wishing and not action. These same people suffer for their own laziness and lack of strategy. They experience regret and frustration that they don't have what they want. They experience guilt that they don't follow through on anything.

Investing in Yourself

Successful people see the pain of discipline and consistency to achieve excellence and satisfaction as an investment in themselves. If someone came to you and said "You can invest in this opportunity and receive a 30% return on your money, and the risk is very low," you would probably jump on the opportunity.

To not invest in yourself means to experience regret, frustration, guilt, and disappointment. You invest nothing and your return is zero.

If you spend the next five years without doing anything more than spending 8 hours per day at work, and after work just watching t.v. or relaxing, you will have nothing to show for it.

If you spend those same five years training, you will earn rank and develop abilities that others don't have. You put yourself in the top 10% of all martial artists. You will be in shape, confident, less stressed than you were if you hadn't trained, you treat others better, more self-aware, etc., you may even be an instructor.

You may have even left your nine to five job to put on a gi and make your living as a professional martial arts instructor (you get to choke and armlock people and they pay you for it!)

If you persist, eventually getting your black belt will give you huge returns on the time you put into it.

You can develop the habit of consistency and discipline, which will give you confidence, or of excuses and rationalizing, which will give you regret.

It all depends on your attitude and inner self talk. The average person says "That workout is really hard. I'm older than a lot of these guys, I don't know if this stuff is for me."

The success minded person says "That workout is really hard. This will get me in shape."

The average person says "Work is really busy, and I'm tired, and I have a family. I don't think I have time for this."

The success minded person says, "Work is busy, but I don't live for work. I am tired, but I always feel better during and after I'm done training. I have a family, but this really helps my stress levels and my attitude and I treat them better, plus I'm setting a good example for my spouse and kids to take care of their physical, mental, and emotional health."

Winners make and keep resolutions, and losers make excuses. Winners love discipline, and losers never experience satisfaction of seeing anything through.

Freedom is a choice and slavery is a choice. They are both self-imposed. You can imprison yourself in a life that leaves you empty, or free yourself from the normal day to day routine. The difference is to make the decision to achieve excellence and to keep strengthening your resolve to improve.

Remind yourself what you want and why you want it. If you have a tendency to not follow through on your commitments, change your self talk. Write down your goals, and review them. Brainstorm how to improve your Jiu-Jitsu, and follow through.

If you have a hard time staying with anything, you may be repeating the thoughts of others who hadn't supported you in the past.

"You can't do that. You're not smart enough."

Kill those voices inside and affirm that you are worth it and that you will succeed. Your subconscious will believe whatever you repeat to yourself over and over. Resolve to keep improving yourself daily.

APPENDIX B

Meditation Techniques

"You may control a mad elephant; you may shut the mouth of the bear and the tiger; ride the lion and play with the cobra; by alchemy you may earn your livelihood; you may wander through the universe incognito; make vassals of the gods; be ever youthful; you may walk on water and live in fire; but control of the mind is better and more difficult."

-Thayumanavar, saint from South India

Meditation is the most direct method of developing concentration. The goal is to develop unswerving concentration and calmness while you train and in your daily life.

Jean Jacques Machado speaks about this state of concentration where he is on auto pilot. His mind and emotions does not get in the way of his flow.

Rickson Gracie speaks about the same state- a state of calmness without mental or emotional tension where he is intensely aware of his partner and his own body, and he can move freely without limitation.

Preliminary Exercises

These can be done from one to five minutes before you begin meditating:

1. Triangular breathing: breathe in for a count of twenty, hold for twenty, exhale for twenty.

2. Breathe in deeply and tense your whole body; exhale and relax.

3. Consciously relax each major muscle in your body.

4. Hands up and in breathing: start with your arms straight out in front of your shoulders. Breathe in and bring your hands toward your stomach, palms down and hands still the same distance apart. As your lungs fill up, bring your hands up to your shoulders. Exhale and straighten your arms out back to the original position in front of your shoulders.

5. Vijay breath: breathe in and out quickly and make an aspirated sound in your nose. Do for one minute then breathe calmly or do another technique.

6. Stretch and breathe deeply as if the oxygen is going into the muscles.

Meditation techniques

All sitting meditation techniques require that your spine be straight and eyes half or completely closed. You may sit cross legged or one a chair.

Lying on your back often leads people to sleep, and sleep is not meditation!

Meditation requires that you be very focused and very still. Remember that in meditation, the body is a distraction. You are trying to calm the body so it does not get in the way of your focus.

Paramahansa Yogananda, a sage from India who taught meditation, likened the senses to telephones. Trying to concentrate while you have the input of hearing, feeling, taste, sight, and smell is like having five telephones ringing at once. Reduce the volume of these telephones and you will develop great peace and relaxation.

Techniques of Meditation

1. Once you get to a state of relaxation and calmness after doing the preliminary exercises, concentrate on the peace. Settle into it. If you mind starts getting restless, go back to doing one of the preliminary exercises.

2. Watch the breath without controlling it.

3. Listen to peaceful or inspiring music with deep concentration.

4. Choose a quality you want to develop in yourself- confidence, relaxation, happiness, whatever you like.

Close your eyes and visualize your face and body while you are in this desired state. Press you thumb to your first finger for three seconds, programming yourself by associating the desired state with this "trigger" of pressing your thumb to your first finger.

Now visualize yourself moving in an activity while in this state (like rolling). Press your thumb and first finger again. Now try to feel the desired state in your body.

Press your thumb and forefinger again. You are associating a certain feeling with a physical action- maybe relaxation with pressing your thumb and forefinger.

This technique is like installing a button on yourself. Every time you press the button you feel some degree of that feeling. This technique has been used successfully by Olympic athletes to perform at high levels under pressure.

5. Repeat the word "home" softly or mentally. Think of home as a place of relaxation and peace.

6. Listen to the aspirated sound of the breath as you inhale and exhale.

7. Visualize a light or a color in your body and the light or color withdrawing into your spine and your brain.

The Tea Ceremony

Toyotomi Hideyoshi was a great Japanese warlord. One of Hideyoshi's vassals thought that he was spending too much time with Sen no Rikyu, a great tea instructor, instead of military strategy.

He decided to assassinate the tea master. He invited him over to tea. The vassal pulled out a dagger as the tea master had his back turned to him. The vassal saw that the tea master was so focused that there was no time for him to attack and realized why Hideyoshi was studying tea- to learn to concentrate deeply and control the mind.

APPENDIX C

List of Basics I Know

Mount Defense

1.

2.

3.

Mount Attacks

1.

2.

3.

Guard Attacks

1.

2.

3.

Guard Passes

1.

2.

3.

Side Mount Defense

1.

2.

3.

Side Mount Attacks

1.

2.

3.

Back Defense

1.

2.

3.

Back Attacks

1.

2.

3.

Made in the USA
Middletown, DE
22 January 2018